Contents

About badminton

Badminton is a racket game played by two players (**singles**) or four players (**doubles**). It combines some of the powerful **overhead** strokes of tennis with some of the strokes played in squash. Players aim to volley a shuttlecock back and forth over a 1.55 metre high **net**. A **rally** continues until one player is unable to return the shuttle over the net.

Points can only be scored by the serving side. If the non-serving side win a rally, they gain **service**, but the score is not changed. Service commences from the right-hand service area, and the shuttle is hit to the diagonally opposite service area. If the server wins the rally, a point is scored and he or she moves to the left-hand court. The server alternates from side to side for as long as he or she continues to win points.

In doubles and men's singles, a game is won by the first player or team to reach 15 points. In women's singles a game is won by the first player to reach 11 points. The winner of the match is the player or pair who first wins two games.

At top level, players require the agility of a gymnast and the reflex speed of a fencer. Badminton is a unique game in that, at one moment, a player might hit the shuttle at up to 260 kilometres per hour, and the next moment play a delicate shot with millimetre perfect accuracy.

A badminton doubles game in progress

UK highlights

Badminton is widely played in the United Kingdom, and with 53,010 registered players, the UK ranks tenth in the world. The Far-East country of Taiwan has the highest number of registered players, with over 612,000, and over 100 million people play badminton worldwide.

England was one of the nine countries that founded the International Badminton Federation (IBF) in 1934.

There are now 138 affiliated countries. The All-England Championship is the oldest and most famous badminton tournament in the world.

Fastest smash

Badminton is officially the world's fastest racket sport. Simon Archer of England features in the *Guinness Book of Records* with a smash recorded at 260 kph (November 1996).

Simon Archer and Chris Hunt competing in the men's doubles at the All-England Championship.

Honoured by the Queen

Gillian Clark of England had a distinguished badminton career and is now a television commentator. She was awarded an MBE by the Queen in 1996.

UK news

- Darren Hall has been UK national champion 16 times.
- Kelly Morgan (Wales) recently made history when she became the first UK ladies' singles player to reach the top ten in the world rankings.
- English men's doubles Chris Hunt and Simon Archer achieved number 2 in the world rankings (1998).
- English women's doubles Joanne Goode and Donna Kellogg were ranked 5th in the world (1998).
- Scottish mixed doubles Kenny and Elinor Middlemiss ranked 13th in the world (1998).
- 1998 England coach, Park Joo Bong (Korea), won a gold medal in the men's doubles in badminton's first Olympics at Barcelona in 1992. He also won silver in the mixed doubles in the 1996 Olympics held at Atlanta.

Commonwealth success

At the 1998 Commonwealth Games in Malaysia:

- The English women's badminton team won a gold medal.
- English mixed doubles Archer and Goode won gold; England also won silver and bronze medals.
- Kelly Morgan (Wales) won gold in the ladies' singles.
- English women's doubles Kellogg and Goode won gold.

World news: the Indonesian player Susi Susanti is a badminton legend. Winner of nearly every major title, she has recently announced her retirement.

History of badminton

The name badminton comes from the name of the Duke of Beaufort's country house at Badminton in England. An early version of the game is thought to have been developed by guests at the Duke's house in 1870. It was based on children's games known as battledore and shuttlecock.

In the 1870s, the game became very popular with British Army officers in India, where it was called '**poona**'.

The International Badminton Federation

In 1893 the Badminton Association of England was formed. It produced the first set of formal rules. The governing body today is the International Badminton Federation, which was founded in 1934.

A game of shuttlecock. This illustration was drawn in the 1850s.

Badminton was popular among the British in India. This illustration was drawn in 1874.

The oldest and most famous badminton tournament in the world is the All England Championships. Played in Birmingham each March, this tournament dates back to 1899. It consistently boasts the world's highest ranked male and female competitors.

Contested every two years, the World Championships for men and women were first played in 1977. Badminton has been a Commonwealth Games event since 1966. It became an official Olympic Sport at the Barcelona Games in 1992. Badminton is played passionately throughout South-East Asia, and is the national sport of Malaysia.

What you need to play

Badminton is usually played indoors on a non-slip wooden surface. The game may be played outside, but the lightness of the **shuttlecock** can make play quite difficult in even a light breeze.

The court

The court is 13.4 metres long by 6.10 metres wide. The net is made from a light mesh and is supported at each side by 1.52 metre high net posts. Shots are often played very high so there should be a clear space of 9 metres above the court.

Singles and doubles games are played on the same court, but using different boundary lines and service areas.

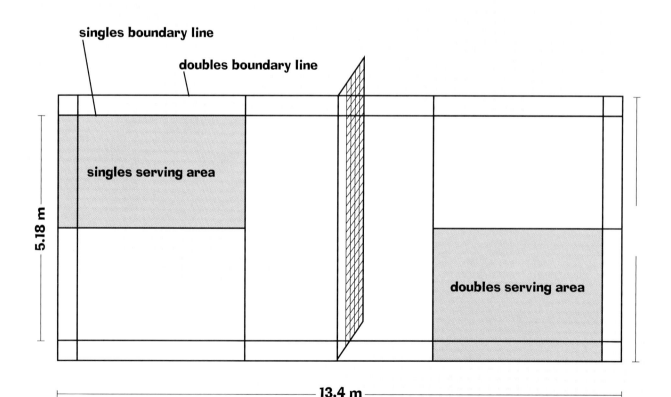

singles boundary line

doubles boundary line

singles serving area

doubles serving area

5.18 m

13.4 m

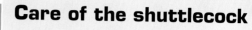

The racket

The racket is usually made from carbon graphite or metal. Rackets for junior players weigh between 85 and 100 grams. When choosing a racket, make sure it has a comfortable grip. As a general guide, your fingers should be about 5 millimetres from the palm of your hand when you hold the racket in the forehand grip.

The shuttlecock

The shuttlecock (or shuttle) is badminton's 'ball'. It is very light and fragile, but it travels fast through the air because of its aerodynamic shape. A shuttle weighs just 4.8 grams. There are two types of shuttle: the original feathered variety and the newer synthetic variety. More expensive and fragile the feathered variety are composed of 16 goose feathers set into a base of domed cork. The feathered shuttle is most commonly used in competition by skilled players. As a beginner the less expensive synthetic shuttle is fine.

Players wear shorts and a shirt with well-cushioned shoes.

Clothing

Players wear shorts, shirts, socks and shoes. The material should be absorbent and loose fitting to allow freedom of movement.

Shoes are the most important component of your kit. Badminton is a game requiring great speed. Your shoes should be light and flexible. The soles must provide excellent grip as you stop, start and turn regularly at top speed.

Rules

Before play begins, opposing sides toss a coin. The winning side chooses either to serve or to receive, or to play at a particular end of the court.

Scoring

A standard match consists of the best of three games, each of which is played to 15 points. Women's singles consist of the best of three games played to 11 points.

A point is scored for each rally won by the serving player or side. Only the serving side can add a point to its score. If you serve and lose that rally, your opponent gains the serve and the opportunity to score.

Serving

The service must always be underarm with the racket pointing downwards. The shuttle must be struck when it is below waist height. Both feet must be on the floor and within the service area. The receiver must remain still with both feet on the ground until the shuttle is struck.

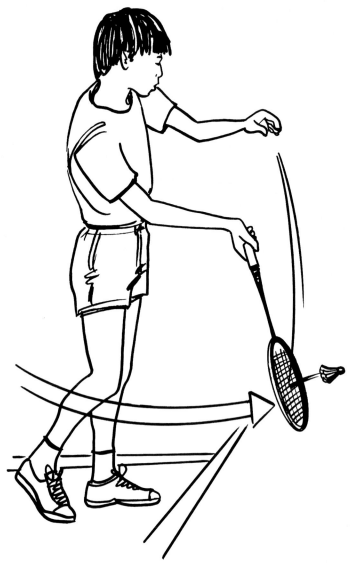

The correct service action. The serve is underarm, and the racket is pointing downwards.

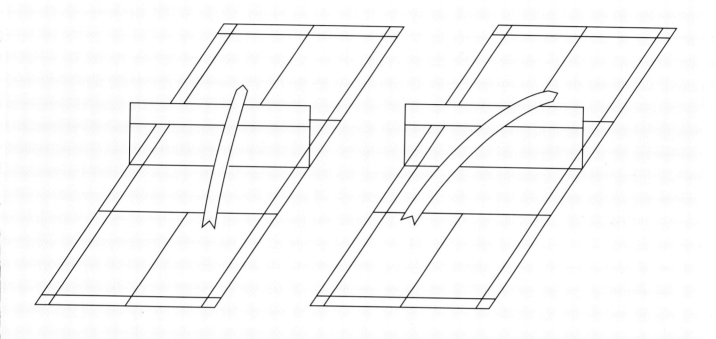

The first serve is taken from the right-hand side.

Subsequent serves are taken from the right-hand area when the server's score is even.

When the server's score is odd, he or she serves from the left-hand service area.

Players must always serve into the service area diagonally opposite. The first service of the game is taken from the right-hand service court. You continue to serve until you lose a rally, alternating between right and left service courts.

Doubles serving

In doubles, each pair has two chances with the serve, except at the beginning of the game when they have just one service chance.

When a pair gains service from their opponents, they commence serving from the right-hand service court. When the first player loses the service, it becomes his or her partner's turn to serve. When the second player loses the serve, the service then passes to their opponents.

In doubles, the receiving pair doesn't change sides when the service passes between their opponents.

Rules

Winning and losing points

Players must always hit the shuttle before it hits the floor. If the shuttle lands on your side of the court, the rally ends and either you lose service or your opponent gains a point. If the shuttle is hit by your opponent and lands outside your court, the rally ends and either you gain a point or win the service.

Likewise, if a rally is stopped because the shuttle doesn't clear the net, a point is awarded to the side not at fault, or they gain the service.

There are other ways that a rally may end, resulting in loss of service or a point to your opponent:

- striking the shuttle before it passes over the net
- touching the net with racket or body, while the shuttle is in play

If a player reaches over the net to play a shot, he or she will lose service, or a point will be awarded to the other side.

In or out?

A shuttle falling on the line is considered 'in court'. It must fall completely clear of the line to be called 'out'.

- putting any part of your body under the net
- hitting the shuttle twice – either by the one player in singles, or once each by both players in doubles
- an incorrect serving action
- missing the shuttle when you are serving
- the shuttle does not clear the net
- the shuttle touches the side walls or the ceiling.

The umpire

One umpire controls the badminton match. He or she sits in a chair above one side of the net. The umpire announces the game score after each point and the set score at the end of each game.

Let

The umpire may call '**let**' for an accidental or unforeseen occurrence which stops play; for example, when a shuttle from another court disturbs play. When a let occurs, play stops and the player who served the rally repeats his or her service.

Unlike tennis, if the shuttle touches and then passes over the net when it is served, the point is played out normally.

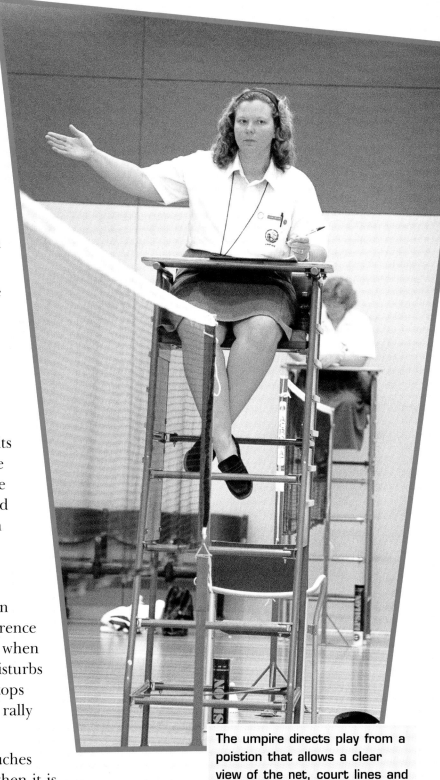

The umpire directs play from a poistion that allows a clear view of the net, court lines and the players.

Skills

Badminton players aim to win points by playing the shuttle over the net into a spot where the opponent cannot return it, or hitting a shot that is difficult to return, forcing your opponent to make an error.

Badminton demands quick movement. Keep your eye on the shuttle and respond quickly as the shuttle leaves your opponent's racket strings. Good balance and fast movements are important. Short, sharp steps and lunges are essential.

Fast reflexes and long stretches are important skills for badminton.

Flicking the wrist forward and downwards as the racket makes contact gives extra speed to the shuttle.

The use of the arm, forearm and wrist

The arm is where the speed of the shuttle is generated. In all power strokes bend your arm fully, and then with a strong throwing action push your arm straight. You can use your wrist to add further power by using a flicking motion as you hit the shuttle. For a forehand shot, bend your wrist back and flick it forward powerfully on impact with the ball. The same principle applies to the backhand shot.

Hold the shuttlecock gently between your thumb and first finger.

Skills

Gripping the racket

To make the most of your strokes, your grip must be correct. Gripping the racket too tightly will restrict wrist movement. There are two main types of grip: the forehand grip and the backhand grip. Practise each one and then practise changing from one to the other so that your grip changes will be smooth and fast in a game.

The forehand grip

This is the beginner's most basic grip. All shots on the racket side of the body are played with the forehand grip.

Hold the racket in your non-playing hand. Now place your playing hand flat on the strings with your wrist towards the racket handle. Slide this hand down the handle until it reaches the grip. Imagine shaking hands with the grip so that a V forms between your thumb and forefinger. Curl your fingers around the grip.

The forehand grip

Start with your playing hand flat on the strings of the racket to form the forehand grip.

The backhand grip

To play backhand shots with control and power, you need to change your grip to the backhand grip.

From the forehand grip, relax your fingers. Turn the racket about 30 degrees clockwise (anticlockwise if you are left-handed) so that your thumb is placed on the flatter side of the grip. Your thumb now provides control of the stroke.

The ready position

After each stroke in a singles rally, you should re-position yourself roughly in the centre of the court so that you can then move to any part of the court to receive your opponent's next shot. This position is called the **base position**.

Stand with your racket held at chest height and slightly forward. Keep your knees slightly bent and your weight on the balls of your feet.

The backhand grip. The racket is rotated so that the thumb is against the flatter side of the grip.

Skills

Serving

Each serve sends the shuttle on a different flight path. The first two are used mainly in doubles matches.

The low serve

Your aim with the low serve is to give the shuttle the flattest possible flight. It starts its drop just before clearing the top of the net, and should clear it by just millimetres. Such a low flight will prevent your opponent from lunging forward and striking the shuttle back forcefully down over the net. He or she will have to hit the shuttle upwards to return it, and this will give you the chance to respond with a strong attacking shot.

Stand side-on to the net. With a forehand grip, drop the shuttle, simultaneously bringing the racket forward to make impact just in front of, and below, your waist. Push the shuttle over the net with the racket, rather than trying to strike it hard. The shuttle should travel just over the net, and land on, or just over, your opponent's front service line.

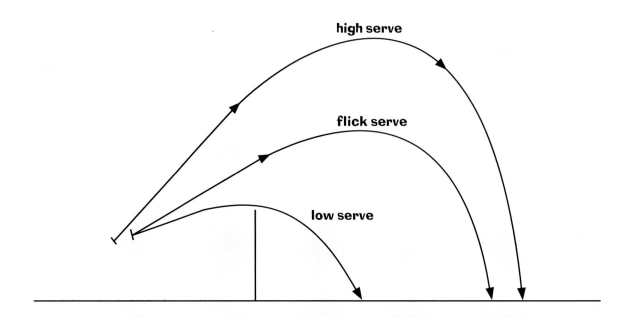

For the low serve and the flick serve, position yourself close to the centre line and the front of the service area. For the high serve, stand about 1–1.5 metres further back.

The high serve

Used mainly in singles matches, the aim of the high serve is to force your opponent deep into the back court from where it is difficult to return with an attacking shot. This serve should be aimed at the back line.

Hold the racket with a forehand grip and your wrist back. Bring your racket arm and shoulder back before you swing your shoulder forward, quickly straightening your wrist just before impact.

Follow through with the racket shoulder raising the racket to net height. Then move quickly back to the base position in the centre of the court.

Follow your swing through to bring the racket to net height for the high serve.

The flick serve

The **flick** serve is very similar to the low serve. It is used to deceive your opponent as he or she will prepare to receive a low serve and not be prepared for the serve that follows.

For the flick serve, start with the same stance and stroke as for the low serve. Just before the racket makes contact with the shuttle, flick your wrist. The shuttle will be sent high over the receiver's head, landing just in front of the rear service line.

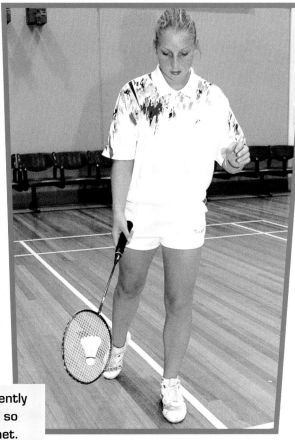

Drop the shuttle and gently push it with the racket so that it just clears the net.

Skills

Forehand strokes

Most badminton shots are played overhead. There are three main overhead strokes played with the forehand grip:

- the clear
- the drop shot
- the smash.

The clear

The **clear** is a defensive stroke used to send the shuttle high and deep to the back line of your opponent's court. From a position at the back of the court, strike the shuttle in an upward direction so that it travels in a high arc to drop vertically near the back line.

Positioned side-on and with your weight on your back foot, extend your racket behind and above your head. Step forward as the shuttle drops, extending your racket forwards. Strike the shuttle high, above your playing shoulder, then follow through strongly.

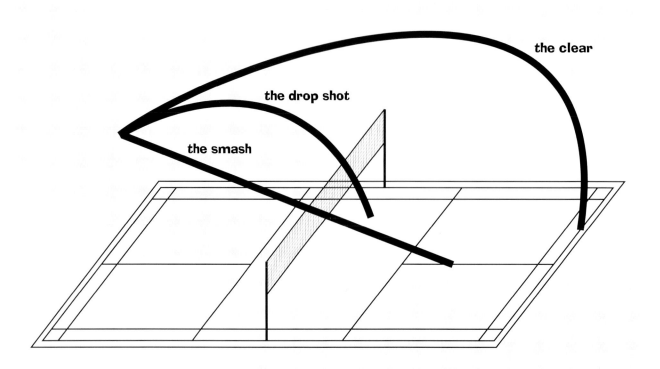

The drop shot

The **drop shot** is an attacking shot that is played delicately. Approach the shuttle as if you are about to drive forcefully to your opponent who is standing mid-court. Then, at the last moment, slow your racket and hit the shuttle gently.

The shuttle will drop just over the net, forcing your opponent to lunge forward to try to hit it. If he or she is unable to return your drop shot, then his or her forward lunge will have left a large unguarded area mid-court into which you will be able to return the shuttle.

The smash

The **smash** is the power stroke that often closes the rally. It is played with a similar action to that of the clear and the drop. Your aim when smashing is to hit down fast to beat your opponent. Aim to hit the shuttle so that it hits the floor just inside and midway along the sideline.

Position yourself a little further behind the shuttle as you will strike it earlier, when it is about 30 centimetres in front of you. At impact, bend your wrist powerfully forward to bring the racket head downwards.

Jump up to give yourself the height to play the smash down powerfully over the net.

Follow through powerfully after the smash.

Skills

Backhand strokes

There are two main backhand strokes in badminton: the backhand **lift** and the backhand overhead clear. For each one, make sure you are using the correct backhand grip. (See page 19.)

The backhand lift

The backhand lift is an underhand stroke which is used to return a low shuttle from the front of the court. Your aim is to hit the shuttle high and deep – giving you time to return to the base position in the centre of the court.

Take a long lunge forward as you take your racket back to your opposite shoulder with your wrist bent back.

Swing the racket forward to make contact at arm's length in front of you.

Continue the swing upwards, straightening your wrist. Follow through, taking the racket up above head height.

Take your racket
above and just
behind your head.

The backhand
overhead clear

The backhand
overhead clear is played
in reponse to high shots
to your backhand side. As
you stretch up to the
shuttle, turn your back to
the net. Extend your arm and flick your
wrist to send the shuttle back over your
shoulder and over the net.

Strike the shuttle early, above and
slightly to the side of your head
without any follow through. Direct
the shuttle to the back of the court.
Return quickly to the base position.

Net shots

Net shots are played from
a position up close to the
net – closer than the service
line. These strokes are aimed
just to clear the net and land
in your opponent's forecourt.

Step forward with your racket
foot striking the shuttle high
and early, pushing the shuttle
so that it just clears the net.
Once you have played the shot
return quickly to the base
position.

Gently push the
shuttle over the net.

Skills

The block

As a beginner, the first defensive shot you will learn is the block. If you are receiving a powerful attacking stroke, such as a smash, with the shuttle hit to one side of your body, you will have little time for backswing.

Position yourself at mid-court almost square to the net with one foot slightly forward. With a backhand grip, place your racket slightly to the backhand side. With a locked wrist and your racket head tilted slightly up, push it forward to block the shuttle so that it rebounds back over the net. The shuttle should strike your racket and then skim off it, to land just over the net.

Concentrate hard on the shuttle as your opponent serves.

Returning serve

Your return of serve is very important for your position throughout the rally. A strong return may result in an outright win or may at least put you into a commanding position. A weak return will leave you under pressure. Hit the shuttle downwards from its highest point. Don't wait for the shuttle – by striking it early you will put your opponent under immediate pressure.

As your partner prepares to serve, stand ready to return. With your knees slightly bent, stand with your non-racket foot slightly forward and your weight evenly balanced on both feet. Hold your racket in front of, and just above, your face. Be ready to move quickly in any direction to return with a powerful shot.

Where to stand when returning serve

When returning serve in doubles, stand close to the front of the area and near the centre line. In singles, stand almost in the centre of your serving box.

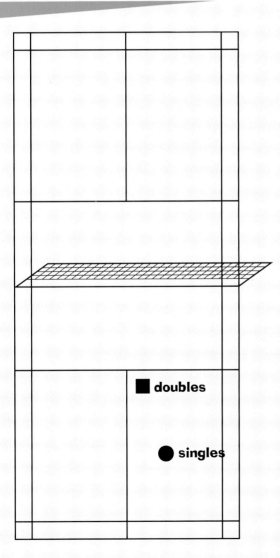

■ **doubles**

● **singles**

Always try to hit the shuttle at its highest point.

Getting ready

Before playing or practising it is important that you stretch and warm up your muscles. A thorough warm-up will help to prevent injuries. It will improve your flexibility and prepare your body for more vigorous activity.

Shoulder stretch
Stretch one arm straight across your body. Use your other hand to pull your elbow in to your chest until you feel the stretch.

Lower back stretch
Lie on your back with your legs outstretched. Bend one knee up to your chest and lift your head and shoulders off the floor to meet it.

Side bends
Stand upright with one hand on your waist. Bring your other arm up and over your head as you bend to the side. Make sure you don't lean forward as you bend. Hold the stretch for about 10 seconds and then stretch the other side.

Neck stretch
Gently pull your head towards your shoulder until you feel the stretch. Repeat the same stretch on the other side.

Arm stretch
Bend and lift your
arm behind your head
and gently push your
elbow down with your
other hand.

Calf stretch
Stand with one foot in front
of the other. Lean forward so
that your weight is on your
front foot. Bend your
leading leg and lean
forward, keeping
both feet flat on
the floor. Hold the
stretch for about
10 seconds and
then stretch
the other leg.

Arm circles
Stretch your arms
above your head
and take them
around in circles
forwards and then
backwards, stretching
as far up and around
as you can.

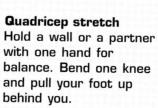

Quadricep stretch
Hold a wall or a partner
with one hand for
balance. Bend one knee
and pull your foot up
behind you.

Taking it further

Useful addresses

The Badminton Association of England/
The English Schools Badminton Assoc.
National Badminton Centre
Bradwell Road
Loughton Lodge
Milton Keynes MK8 9LA
☎ 01908 268400

The Scottish Badminton Union
Cockburn Centre
40 Bogmoor Place
Glasgow G51 4TQ
☎ 0141 445 1218

The Scottish Schools Badminton Union
The Shieling
Brownsburn Road
Airdrie ML6 9QG
☎ 01236 760943

The Welsh Badminton Union
4th Floor, Plymouth Chambers
3 Westgate Street
Cardiff CF1 1DD
☎ 01222 222082

The Badminton Union of Ireland
Baldoyle Badminton Centre
Baldoyle Industrial Estate
Grange Road
Baldoyle
Dublin 13
☎ 003531 839 3028

The International Badminton Federation
Manor Park Place
Rutherford Way
Cheltenham GL51 9TU
☎ 01242 234904

The European Badminton Union
Vluyner Platz 7+8,
D-47799
Krefeld
Germany
☎ 0049 2151 503020

There is currently no Welsh Schools
Badminton Association, and The
Badminton Union of Ireland deals with
Irish Schools Badminton.

Further reading

Know the Game: Badminton, A & C Black Publishers, London, 1994
Davis, P. *Badminton – Play the Game*, Cassell Publishers, London, 1998
Edwards, J. *Crowood Sports Guides – Badminton Techniques, Tactics & Training*
Crowood Publishers, Wiltshire, 1997
Roper, P. *The Skills of the Game: Badminton*, Crowood Publishers, Wiltshire, 1995

Glossary

base position the mid-court area a player returns to between playing shots

clear a stroke which sends the shuttle high and deep to drop vertically at the back of the opponent's court

doubles where two players play as a team to compete against an opposition pair

drop shot hitting the shuttle softly so that it just drops over the net

flick played with a short backswing and little follow through, the ideal flick will travel just over and above your opponent's outstretched racket

let a let is called when a point needs to be re-played

lift a defensive stroke where the shuttle travels above your opponent's racket to land at the rear of the court

net the court is divided into two by a 1.55 metre high net

overhead a shot played from above the head. The majority of shots are played overhead with forehand or backhand strokes.

rally a number of hits between players

poona the name given to the game when first invented by British army officers in India

service the shot that commences each rally

shuttlecock a small cork base with feathers inserted into it, also known as the shuttle. The shuttlecock is hit back and forth across the net in a game of badminton.

singles when one player opposes another in a game of badminton

smash a powerful attacking overhead stroke that causes the shuttle to head straight for the ground in your opponent's court

Index